Ginbot 7 Ethiopian National Election and Its Aftermath: How and Why The 2005 Democratic Election in Ethiopia Turned Violent

Teferi Fantahun

For ebook visit Amazon.com or smashwords.com

Also by Teferi Fantahun

Reflection on Violence☹ War ☹ and Peace☺: A New and Early Approach to Violence Prevention

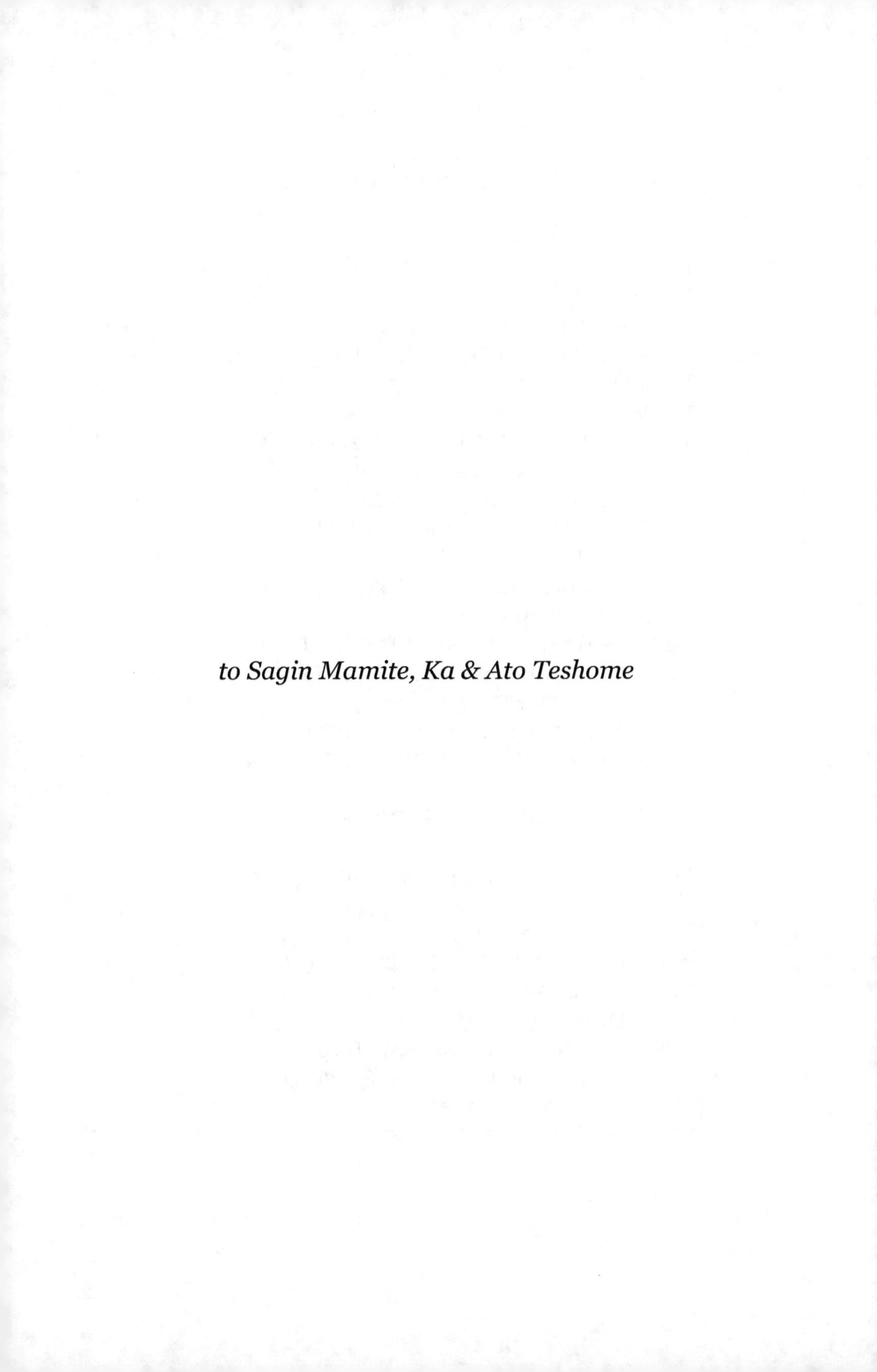

to Sagin Mamite, Ka & Ato Teshome

TABLE OF CONTENTS

ABSTRACT

The purpose of this research was to explore, describe, interpret, and analyze factors that contributed to Ethiopia's post-election-day political crisis, using Africa's transitions to democracy as a context. By looking closely into the process by which Ethiopia became a "federal democratic republic," and the country's political trouble following the May 2005 national election and its crisis-ridden aftermath, this study has attempted to uncover the interaction of the significant factors involved. Unraveling and uncovering the anatomy of a political system that has been taking root in Ethiopia since the 1990s and understanding the present political situation is the focal point of this study.

Using Dahl's (1971) eight criteria and Ethiopia's 1994 constitution, this study attempted to identify the behaviors exhibited by both the ruling and opposition parties before and after the May 15, 2005 Ethiopian election.
As this study suggests, the 2005 election may be indicative of a trend that has been taking place in Africa's new democracies. This trend is toward abandoning democratic principles, as we know it in the West, for a more convenient form of non-liberal electoral or pseudo-democracy, or the embrace of authoritarian systems of government.

INTRODUCTION AND STATEMENT OF RESEARCH QUESTION

The purpose of this research was to explore, describe, interpret, and analyze factors that contributed to Ethiopia's post-election day political crisis, following the May 15, 2005 national election. By looking closely into the process by which Ethiopia became a federal democratic republic, and the country's political trouble following that election, this study aimed at uncovering the interactions of the significant factors that led to the violence that followed the election. It is important to note at the outset of this study that it addressed only the national parliamentary election that took place in May 2005.

The 1990s have seen several of Africa's most notorious dictators removed from power. Some of the processes by which these dictators were removed from power were nonviolent, while others were extremely violent.

Ethiopia is currently at a political crossroads. The 2005 national election provided an opportunity to transform Ethiopia into a democratic republic, but the major political parties lost it on mistrust, negative perceptions, and miscalculations. On May 15, 2005 nearly twenty-six million Ethiopians went to the 35,000 polling stations across the country to participate in their country's first truly democratic national election, according to the National election Board of Ethiopia (NEBE,

2005). Many people waited in line for more than six hours to cast their ballots.

The major political parties that competed for national offices were the ruling Ethiopian People's Revolutionary Democratic Front (EPRDF), the Coalition for Unity and Democracy (CUD), and the United Ethiopian Democratic Forces (UEDF).

For the first time, the Ethiopian people were given the opportunity to participate in their political process freely. As a result, the election attracted 1845 candidates, representing 35 political parties, and including 353 independent candidates, all of which were contending for seats in the House of People's Representatives, according to the NEBE (2005).

On May 16, 2005, a day after the election, the EPRDF, the ruling party, announced that it had won the national election. The announcement was made while the NEBE was still counting votes, according to the European Union Election Observation Commission (2005). It took the NEBE more than three months to confirm EPRDF's electoral victory. On May 20, 2005 the Coalition for Unity and Democracy (CUD), a coalition of four political parties published a press release that announced the formation of its North American office. Around this time, the CUD suggested its own "huge victory," which would allow the party to form a government (CUD, 2005). By publicly claiming or suggesting electoral victory ahead of the

NEBE, the leaders of the EPRDF and CUD escalated the conflict and mistrust between the leadership and supporters of the two parties.

To the surprise of many, these leaders cornered themselves and eventually surrendered their leadership positions to key constituents and were forced to engage in the difficult tasks of intra-party and inter-party negotiations to overcome the post-election crisis. Party officials held town hall meetings both inside and outside Ethiopia in an attempt to address the post-election crisis. The crisis had created political confusion, uncertainty, and tense political environments compounded by fear and mistrust between and among leaders and supporters of the EPRDF and CUD. It also replaced the hope and optimism that characterized the pre-election period.

Two additional actions by the late Prime Minister Meles Zenawi added tension to an already tense situation. Following allegations of fraud by the opposition parties, the prime minister ordered a one-month ban on demonstrations. He also took control of the security forces in Addis Ababa, Ethiopia's capital. These actions provoked a series of emotionally charged protests in Addis Ababa and in other parts of the country.

The EPRDF's regime responses to the protesters in Addis Ababa brought a massive and an emotional reaction from the Ethiopian expatriate communities around the world. In one positive outcome, EPRDF managed to bring together the divided Ethiopian communities and the major political parties. Today, there are several Ethiopian pro-democracy groups outside Ethiopia providing financial and political support to the opposition parties.

The Problem

In line with donors' expectations, Ethiopia had been holding periodic democratic elections since 1992 (NEBE, 2005). Even so, the implementation of free and fair elections in Ethiopia continued to be far from being reasonably acceptable to all parties.

In the aftermath of Ginbot 7 national election, the leaders of the main opposition party— CUD—were all sent to prison. The government charges the opposition leaders of treason and attempted genocide. In addition, the ruling party managed to silence the independent media, and several editors of independent newspapers were accused of treason and attempted genocide and were sent to prison or are in exile.

Certainly, the political crisis that began on May 16, 2005 is not over yet. The struggle for self government and citizenship in Ethiopia has continues even to this day. The type of struggle the opposition leaders and their supporters would undertake is not totally clear yet. Whichever forms of struggle the political actors decide to pursue will have far-reaching consequences not only for Ethiopia, but also for the entire East and Horn of African region. This is especially true, if the political leaders in Ethiopia decide to settle their political differences through violent means, which appears to be a more likely scenario, considering the political tradition of the country.

In light of the previous discussion, this research will attempt to answer the following main and sub-questions:

Main research question:

• What factors contributed to the post-election day political crisis in Ethiopia because of the May 2005 national election?

The following sub-questions will help me answer the main research question:

• How and why did the May 2005 Ethiopian national election turn violent?
• How did the ruling and main opposition parties respond to the post-election day crisis?
• What role, if any, did the donor communities play during the crisis?
• How did Ethiopians at home and abroad react to the political crisis?

DEMOCRACY AND THE RULE OF LAW: CONCEPTUAL FRAMEWORK

In today's world, there are multiple forms of democracies. Defining such complex concepts as democracy is a daunting task, and there is no agreement among political scientists on one definition of democracy. Robert A. Dahl (1971) proposed eight criteria in his book, Polyarchy, that are the most salient features of democracy.

These features include:
- ✓ The right to vote,
- ✓ The right to be elected,
- ✓ The right of political leaders to compete for support and votes,
- ✓ Elections that are free and fair,
- ✓ Freedom of association,
- ✓ Freedom of expression,
- ✓ Alternative sources of information, and
- ✓ Institutions for making public policies depend on vote and other expressions of preferences. (in Lijphart, 1999, p. 49)

The aforementioned criteria have been the main features of many third wave democracies. Huntington (in Diamond, 1999) defined third wave democracies as those democracies, which have formed since 1974. Ethiopia's 1994 constitution contains many, if not all, of Dahl's proposed criteria. For example, under article 38 of Ethiopia's constitution, every Ethiopian national has the right to "vote and to be elected." Article 29 stipulates, "everyone has the right to freedom of expression without interference. The right shall include freedom to seek, receive and impart information and ideas of all kinds, regardless of frontiers, either orally, in writing or in print, in the form of art, or through any media of his [or her] choice" (Ethiopian constitution, 1994).

Among the many features of old and new democracies has been political contestation for public office and the public's participation in the electoral process. However, in both old and new democratic counties, free and fraudulent-free elections have become more and more of a challenge. The failure of elections officials and election observers to administer free and fair elections in many Third Wave democracies has made the democratic process incomplete and election-related conflict inevitable.

Using Dahl's eight criteria and the Ethiopia's 1994 constitution, this study attempted to identify the behaviors exhibited by both the ruling and opposition parties before and after the May 15, 2005 election in a balanced, but critical, manner. In so doing, I have made my utmost effort to be fair and balanced as I have described and interpreted the case. I have also attempted to assess the action(s) taken by both the ruling and the main opposition political parties (CUD in particular) in terms of how they have responded to the prevailing political crisis. Applying both Dahl's criteria and empirical democratic theory, I will attempt to provide my readers with a more plausible explanation and hopefully a clearer insight about Ethiopia's post election political crisis; a crisis, which brought an immense misery and suffering to thousands of families.

LITERATURE REVIEW
The Spread of Democracy in Africa

If one takes into account Larry Diamond's (1999) studies of the spread of democracy in Africa, it all began in February 1990 with the sovereign National Conference in Benin, the release of Nelson Mandela, and the lifting of restrictions imposed on the African National Congress by the South African government. By 1997, many of the African states failed to produce democratic systems of governance. As Richard Joseph (1998) observed, "A global intellectual project is under way as scholars [belongs to speculative scholarships] grapple with the mixed nature of many political systems formerly considered to be making a "transition to democracy" (p. 1).

 By 1998, according to Diamond (1999), there were only "seven or nine democratic countries" in the continent. The rest were classified as either pseudo-democracy, one-party or outright authoritarian regimes (p. 2). The question, however, is that to what extent the process in which how Africa began its democratic journey in 1990s explained the crash and the return to non-democratic regimes that followed.

Harbeson (1998) remarked that, Africa's transitions to democracy "will result in democratic progress to the extent that they commence with comprehensive multiparty agreements on the fundamental rules of the game" (p. 43).

Aside from a change in international political context due to the end of the Cold War, the origin, shape, and pace of the African countries' transitions from undemocratic regimes to more democratic regimes has varied considerably between countries. In Ethiopia, the transition to democracy was the outcome of a long and bloody civil war fought between the military junta and its detractors (Berhe, 2005).

Ironically, during Africa's transition to democracy, there had been little confidence in the abilities of the African political elites to construct democratic political systems in their respective countries. The lack of confidence stems from the behavior exhibited by many of Africa's past and present leaders as well as from the "complex interplay of political power, institutions, and social forces" that are historically competitive within African societies (Joseph, 1998, p.1).

In almost every part of Africa, citizens have shown enthusiasm for democracy and a willingness to participate in electoral process if they are given the opportunity. This was evident in South Africa during the first multiethnic elections in 1994, and it was evident in Ethiopia in 2005, when 26 million people participated (NEBE, 2005).

However, as Bratton and Posner's (1999) study

revealed, multiparty elections in Africa have been "far from perfect" (p. 403). According to Harbeson (1998), the quality of the election process in Africa has been in decline since 1995 due to "deliberate interference" by the incumbent political parties in the democratic process in order to secure electoral victory by using control they have in the legislative and executive branches of the government to rewrite the rule that governs election process (p. 43). In spite of adhering to conducting of periodic elections, many African countries have failed to make the election processes free and fair. The failure of many African governments to produce free and fair elections since the continent started moving toward democracy may explain why Africa has been in an ongoing transition from authoritarian to democratic rule.

Since the 1990s, several of Africa's most notorious dictators have been removed from power. Both violent and nonviolent methods were used in these processes. In Ethiopia, a coalition of rebel groups led by the Tigray People's Liberation Front (TPLF) also know locally as *Weyane* defeated the existing military regime and assumed power in Addis Ababa in 1991. For the previous 17 years, a military dictator, Colonel Mengistu Hailemariam, had governed Ethiopia. The end of the Mengistu era and the beginning of EPRDF did not produce the kind of institutional transformation that could effectively regulate the power of the state. Instead, the public has witnessed an entrenched and inaccessible ruling class with unconscious brutality similar to that used by the previous regime of which the current rulers ousted on May 28, 1991 or Ginbot 20, 1984 in Ethiopian calendar.

Similar to the anti-revolutionary campaign of the Mengistu era that terrorized Ethiopian youth, the current Ethiopian government crackdown on the opposition parties, and the mass arrest of Ethiopian youth following the disputed 2005 election was one more indication of the undemocratic actions that the ruling party was willing to take in order to stay in power. As this study suggests, the 2005 election generally may also indicate a general trend that has been taking place in Africa's new democracies. A trend that is clearly also emerging in many new and old democracies around the world: abandoning democracy as we knew it in the West for a more convenient form of non-liberal electoral or pseudo democracy or outright authoritarian systems of government. Carothers (2002) describes the trend as "the end of the transition paradigm" and the consolidation of a "dominant power politics" (p. 11).

Carothers (2002) observed that, with the exception of the Central European and Baltic countries, the majority of third wave democracies have not achieved a well functioning democracy. Most of the third wave democracies are neither dictatorial nor clearly headed to democracy. Instead, they are entering, what Carothers called "a political gray zone" (p. 10).

Among the many gray zones, which Carothers (2002) identified, are the dominant power politics. Carothers argued that countries with dominant power politics permit controlled political space in which citizens may exercise limited political rights. These rights include political contestation by organized political parties as well as freedom of the press. Countries with features of dominant power politics also have, for the most part, the basic democratic institutions, at least in formality. Yet "one political grouping—whether it is a movement, a party, an extended family, or a single leader--dominates the system in such a way that there appears to be little prospect of alternation of power in foreseeable future" (p.11-12).

The EPRDF in Ethiopia used its military, intelligence, and security forces to obstruct a democratic process from taking root in Ethiopia for the last 26 years. The party and its leaders' willingness to use kidnapping, torture, and murder in order to maintain their grip on power has been documented by the Ethiopian Human Rights Council (EHRCO), Amnesty International, Human Rights Watch, and Minority At Risk as well as the U.S. Department of State.

Although the current political trends in Ethiopia as well as in many third wave African countries are creating fear and uneasiness about the future of peace and democracy throughout the continents, Africa's transition to democracy appears to be far from over. From the developmental democracy" perspective that Sklar (1997) suggested, the very presence of legally recognized opposition political parties, as well as the now pretty-well institutionalized periodic elections are important foundations for future development of a democratic political system, whether in Ethiopia or anywhere else.

More importantly, the democratization work that was done by local and international civic organizations since the global resurgence of democracy that started in Latin America in the 1970s have sparked an international movement toward freedom, justice, and democracy. If one pays attention to historical precedents, the human desire and struggle to be free cannot be easily extinguished by way of organized violence, which many new democracies have been willing to use against their own peoples, as the Ethiopian government did since 1991. As the EPRDF's appointed chair of the national election Board of Ethiopia confessed, "The determination of the people to exercise their democratic rights is a sure guarantee that democracy is here to stay (NEBE News, 2005)."

The Transition Paradigm and the Rise of Speculative Scholarship

Since the first half of the 1990s, sub-Saharan African countries witnessed the decline of one-party regimes (Huntington, 1991; Joseph, 1998; Diamond, 1999; Lijphart, 1999; and

Carothers, 2002). The rejection of undemocratic regimes in Africa gave way to the rise and mainstreaming of speculative-scholarship—a form of scholarship that assesses and analyzes political trends in Africa, based merely on speculation and current global political fashion rather than by critically examining the reason as to why such political trends were taking place.

Without putting in a concerted effort to understand the background of an ethnic-based rebel group that has a history of violence and an undemocratic past, Western and some African scholars, along with pro-democracy advocates prematurely characterized a simple mere political regime change in Africa as a "transition from authoritarian rule to democracy."

Harbeson (1998) argued that "the applicability of ...the theoretical literatures on democratic transitions to Africa are at best problematic, reflecting important circumstantial differences between African transitions and antecedent transitions in Europe and the Americas" (p 41).

Carothers (2002) observed that since the 1980s, governmental, quasi-governmental, and nongovernmental organizations (NGOs) were committed to promoting democracy around the world and were actively engaged in many democratization projects in countries considered to be in transition from authoritarian rule to democracy. Confronted with the global surge of democracy during the third wave, pro-democracy groups adopted an analytical model of democratic transitions. This democratic transition model was derived from these organizations' own speculative interpretation of changing political patterns and regime changes that were taking place globally. The model was also influenced by O'Donnell and Schmitter's (1986), work on Latin America transitions from authoritarian rule to democracy.

The "New –breeds" and Africa's Democracy: A Reality Check

Since the early 1990s, based on the unwavering belief in the "new-breeds" of African leaders and their commitment to transform the unfashionable political system of authoritarian and personal rule—that characterized many African countries prior to 1990—the Western leaders and influential members of the donor communities provided generous economic and political support to many African leaders, including the late prime minister of Ethiopia, Meles Zenawi (Van de Walle, 2001). Zenawi, a rebel, and the party he leads, the Ethiopian People's Revolutionary Democratic Front (EPRDF), a rebel movement, "turned democrat" has been the "darling of the international donors" since his movement came to power in 1991 (Lacey, 2005).

Initially, Western support to Mr. Zenawi was conditional. Former U.S. Assistant Secretary of State for African Affairs, Herman Cohen, and the west linked political reform to foreign aid.

The prime minister was informed that the United States would not provide any support to Ethiopia without Zenawi's making a democratic political reform in his country. Cohen's motto was: "No democracy, No cooperation."

Support for the new-breeds came from many streams. Wanting to help establish a just and democratic society in Africa, many idealist, nonprofit organizations have also joined the Western governments and the new African leaders in a massive effort to transform what were once considered to be undemocratic and authoritarian political systems into the new and democratic institutions. As results of such massive efforts put forward by the pro-democracy forces, primarily led by the Western countries and Western Nongovernmental Organizations (WNGO), President Yoweri Moseveni of Uganda, President Isaias Afewerki of Eritrea, President Paul Kagame of Rwanda, and Prime Minster Meles Zenawi of Ethiopia were among the leading new-breed of African leaders who were elevated to a scale almost equivalent to that of a truly great African statesman and freedom fighter, Nelson Mandela of South Africa.

These leaders benefited from their newly found status and Western economic and political support in a time when they needed it the most: during a transition period when the survival of their personal and political movements' future were at constant threat from competing political forces in their respective countries.

In addition, the premature euphoria of positive political and economic trends in Africa has also given an impression that the continent was finally on a truly transformative pathway. South African president Thabo Mbeki characterized these changes as "African renaissance." Mbeki described the notion of renaissance as such characteristics as "self-esteem and self-definition, the dignity of the human being, the material welfare of the individual and the freedom from oppression and fear, cultural and intellectual regeneration," (Lyons, 1991). Such illusionary descriptions of Africa in the 1990s or even in 2017 do not reflect the lived experiences of many Africans.

In Ethiopia, for example, those who are connected with the ruling EPRDF are the primary beneficiaries of the current system. As Belai (2006) wrote, the "members of the inner TPLF circle are...privileged members of the multi-billion-dollar (sic) Endowment Fund for the Rehabilitation of Tigray (EFORT), a chain of 43 companies making up the largest business oligarchy built on the stolen wealth of a starving Ethiopia." Similar views were also held by a majority of this study's participants:

> Ye enesu suwoch becha nachew yetetekemut (People belong to them are the only beneficiaries).

In spite of the reconstituting of a new political

order in Africa, which was also accompanied with a relative peacetime and political stability, Africans have yet to see the phenomenon, which Mbeki characterized, as the African renaissance. The reconstitution of a democratic political order in Africa has been tainted with what the people have thought was a bygone past: political repression, politically-motivated violence, intimidation, mass eviction, torture, assassination, disappearance, arbitrary mass arrest and murder. In Ethiopia, for example, in the aftermath of the disputed May 2005 election and subsequent protest, the ruling EPRDF used post election political crisis as a pretext to round up political opponents, to kill peaceful demonstrators, and prevent a democratic process from taking root in Ethiopia. This was done with the approval of Prime Minister Meles Zenawi and in violation of Article 30 of the 1994 Ethiopian constitution which stipulates that "everyone has the right to assemble and to demonstrate together with others peaceably and unarmed, and to petition" (Ethiopian constitution 1994). Article 18 also provides citizens legal protection from "arbitrary arrest" and detention without charge or conviction (Ethiopian constitution 1994).

Despite an official establishment of a democratic political order in Ethiopia since the 1990s, the "new" order and its operating systems appear to resemble the old. Although the "new system" proclaimed the slogan of democracy and the rule of law, what existed behind the mask of Ethiopia's democracy is the same old dictatorship and a violent one-party rule. As Paxton (2004) remarked, "no dictator rules by himself without obtaining the cooperation of or at least acquiescence of the military, the police, the judiciary, and powerful social and economic forces" (p. 119). In addition, in Africa, no dictator rules without the cooperation of external powers and the most influential political power brokers in African appear to be the Western democracies. However, what remains elusive is where Africa's new democracies are heading: restorations of one man rule, military dictatorship, interethnic or interreligion civil war? The future of democracy in Africa at best is unpredictable to both African and Western scholars. Aside from making comments and suggestions about the difficulties that many Africa's new democracies are facing, no one seems to fully comprehend the complex process of pact-making and alliance-building in multiethnic and multi-religious Africa, along with the ever changing international climate.

Virtually, every African country is multiethnic and multi-religious. Constructing a type of democracy that would be suitable for such diverse communities appears to be a challenge. So far the election-centered democracy that has been promoted in Africa since the 1990s has been flawed, and has had unintended, but grave and destabilizing consequences.

In Ethiopia, in the name of multiparty democracy, the Tigray People's Liberation Front, which is the core of the ERPDF has exploited the ethnic diversity of the Ethiopian society by creating all types of ethnic-based political parties to divide and rule the country.

The proliferation of ethnic-based political parties in Ethiopia since the introduction of multiparty democracy in the 1990s was unprecedented. Today, there are 60 registered ethnic-based and only 17 multiethnic political parties in the country (NEBE, 2005). The deliberate organizing of so many weak, ineffective, and dependent ethnic- based political parties in Ethiopia by the ruling TPLF/EPRDF has rekindled old conflicts and created new ones. The bloody conflict between the Oromo Liberation Front (OLF) and the Oromo People's Democratic Organization (OPDO), a partner with the ruling EPRDF and the heinous crime committed by the OLF against the Amhara peasants in Arusi are some cases in point.

The spread of intra and interethnic violence within a democratic Ethiopia have raised several questions about the effectiveness or merit of promoting ethnic-based political parties to address historic inequality that has existed between the dominant and minority ethnic groups in Ethiopia. To what extent do ethnic political parties help promote the interest of groups they claim to represent? To what extent do ethnic political parties help to promote intra-ethnic or interethnic cooperation and coexistence or vise versa?

Though it was not the purpose of this study to provide answers to these questions, it is safe to say that since the EPRDF came to power, intra and interethnic violence within the FDRE has risen and the southern part of the country has been most affected by interethnic violence. In addition, it is worth noting that the current political system in Ethiopia provides neither individual freedom nor group freedom.

In the absence of political freedom, the tyrannical state prevails. According to Sartori (1987), "The tyrannical state is free to rule at its pleasure, and this means that it deprives its subjects of their freedom" (p. 302).

The above statement is remarkably true and applies to the current political situations in Ethiopia. For the last 26 years, the EPRDF elites have been able to disguise the true anatomy of their repressive and totalitarian regime from the world by officially establishing a "democratic republic" without a democratic credential. As Joseph (1998) points out, "what distinguishes this type of regime is the illusory nature of its democratic institutions and practices, and the fact that they are deliberately contrived to satisfy prevailing international norms of presentability" (p.1).

The crimes committed by the EPRDF security forces for the past 26 years has been meticulously documented by the Ethiopian Human Rights Council (EHRCO), Amnesty International, and Human Rights Watch. The records illustrate that the ruling party was, and is, a tyrannical regime and a willful violator of the human rights of its own citizens. Yet,

Western donors continued to provide economic, military and political support to keep the EPRDF in power.

Abaynesh Wolde, a grieving mother of a teenager killed by Ethiopian security forces in November 2005 told Nolawi Melakedingel, a reporter for the English edition of The Reporter, a weekly magazine published in Addis Ababa:

> I hold this regime responsible for the inhuman measures of its troops. I want justice not from them but from God...They have killed our children they should pay for the cold blood killing they committed. I will only pray to God for he will make that happen.

The government's violent reaction to Ethiopia's post-election-day political crisis and the indiscriminate killing of unarmed civilians in June and November by its security forces only confirmed the undemocratic behavior of the tyrannical one-party state which the Meles regime had been. It also indicated a general trend that has been taking shape in Africa and the world since September 11, 2001.

RESEARCH METHODOLOGY

This study employed a qualitative case study approach. A case study is "an examination of a specific phenomenon such as a program, an event, a person, a process, an institution, or a social group" (Merriam, p.9). I sought and used a qualitative case study design as a technique to understand complex interactions and patterns in a "bounded system," as described by Smith (1978). The bounded system in this study is Ethiopia's post-election-day crisis (the case or phenomenon), which was part of Africa's transition to democracy (the context). In this study the "case" was about Ethiopia's post election political crisis and its aftermath. My main attraction to this approach was that it allows me to use a wide variety of sources of information, including publicly available documents, artifacts, interviews, survey, videos, audios, observations, and informal conversations. As Merriam points out, "Unlike experimental, survey, or historical research, a case study does not claim any particular methods of data collection or data analysis. Any and all methods of gathering data from testing to interviewing can be used in a case study" (p. 10).

Data Collection

This study used multiple data gathering techniques, including issue observations, face-to- face and telephone interviews, email, informal conversations, publicly available documents such as official press releases, political manifestos, research papers, newspapers, online news and publications, and online chat rooms. Secondary resources included books or articles based on primary data or resources, and audiovisual materials that included photographs and videotapes.

The data collected came from multiple sources in order to carry out "constant comparison" of issues as explained by Glaser and Strauss (1967).

I began collecting relevant articles, online publications and press releases in June 2005, when I decided to do my research on Ethiopia's national election. However, I began a more focused data collection in February 2006, which includes interviews and survey and data analysis was completed in September 2006.

The selection of research participants for the interview was predetermined by a specific criteria set by the researcher. Purposive and criterion-based-sampling is used to solve qualitative problems such as "discovering what occurs, the implications of what occurs, and the relationships linking occurrences" (Hoaglin & et al, p. 49). Some of the interview participants were selected by their political or ethnic affiliations. Others participants were selected because of their roles as party officials or participations in the 2005 election as voters.

I conducted semi-structured face-to-face and telephone interviews in the United States with 10 Ethiopian participants. Some of these participants came to the United States after the 2005 election, while others have been long-time residents of the United States. I took handwritten notes of the interviews with the participants for a variety of reasons. First, it seems to me inappropriate to use voice recording devise for security reason and to mark interview participants comfortable, and second, it was easier to protect the participants' anonymity by avoiding the use electronic recording devices. Some of the participants feared that the Ethiopian government would take retaliatory action against them, or their families, if their identity is revealed as study participant.

The biggest challenge to collecting data in Ethiopia was protecting the participants from retaliation from the Ethiopian government. After consulting with potential participants in Ethiopia, we decided to avoid telephone interviews and relied on e-mail instead for our correspondence. Traditional survey questionnaires were prepared and sent to a third-party contact and printed out and distributed to the research participants. The questionnaires were translated into Amharic (Ethiopian national language) for the participants who did not speak English.

The participants came from diverse ethnic, religion, social, educational, and gender backgrounds. All 19 participants live in Addis Ababa, the capital of Ethiopia. I also interviewed two Ethiopian refugees. Thirty-one individuals participated in this study. I asked the participants the following questions:
What factors do you think contributed to the post-election day political crisis in Ethiopia?

1. Why do you think that the 2005 election turned violent?
2. What was your reaction to the outcome of

the election?
3. Politically speaking, what do you think will
happen in Ethiopian in the near future?
4. Politically speaking, what do you want to see
happen in Ethiopia?

Once the participants replied to the above
questions, I sent them follow-up questions to
the aforementioned questionnaire.
There is no established formula for analyzing
interview data of this nature. I used the time-
honored tradition of searching for common
themes among the participants' responses.
According to Stake (1995) this form of data
analysis "gives meaning to first impressions as
well as to final completions (p. 71)."

This technique is similar to building categories
or themes by scanning the data (Merriam,
1988). However, the process of finding patterns
and themes in this study was not limited to
scanning data collected through interviews. I
also closely looked at actions taken by the
EPRDF, the opposition parties, and their
supporters in order to identify recurring
patterns. Using the participants' statements,
along with observation of actions taken by
EPRDF and the opposition parties as data, I
used pattern coding to create themes, identify
patterns, and arrive at possible explanations to
Ethiopia's post election crisis.

In terms of reporting the data in this study, I
integrated what I learned from my study of
publicly available documents such as official
press releases, political manifestos, research

papers, newspapers, online news and publications, with comments from the people I interviewed. Since it was sometimes difficult to make exact translations between Amharic and English, the comments from the participants have been edited according to commonly accepted guidelines for international English. In an attempt to protect the safety and privacy of the participants, no names are used in reporting the responses of the participants. The next chapter is a presentation of data and an analysis of the data collected.

DATA PRESENTATION AND ANALYSIS

A variety of stakeholders in the crisis will be examined in this section. Those stakeholders include: the Ethiopian government, the opposition parties, the Ethiopian diaspora, and donors. Data collected throughout this study will be presented and analyzed.

The Rise of the EPRDF and the Origin of Democracy in Ethiopia

The Ethiopian People's Revolutionary Democratic Front (EPRDF) was established in 1989 by four ethnic based liberation fronts that joined forces to fight the military regime of Colonel Mengistu Hailemariam. The coalition consisted of the Tigray People's Liberation Front (TPLF), the Amhara Nation Democratic Movement (ANDM), the Oromo People's Democratic Organization (OPDO), and the

Southern Ethiopia People's Democratic Movement (SEPDM) (EPRDF, 2005). Among these four rebel groups, the TPLF was the most efficiently organized and heavily armed. In 1991, the EPRDF, along with the Eritrean People's Liberation Front (EPLF) removed the military junta that had ruled Ethiopia for the previous 17 years from power.

In July 1991, the EPRDF, the Oromo Liberation Front (OLF), and other political parties established the Transitional Government of Ethiopia (TGE). In June 1992, the OLF withdrew from TGE because of the intimidation, harassment, and killing of its members and supporters by the EPRDF security forces. The OLF was eventually chased out of the country. The TPLF/EPRDF then quickly used its superior organizational and military might to consolidate power. The TGE, then led by the late Ethiopian Prime Minister, Meles Zenawi, oversaw the establishment of a multiparty democracy and the June 1994 election of the 547-member constituent assembly. Many opposition political parties were either threatened or banned from participating in the 1994 democratic election.

On December 8, 1994, the EPRDF assembly adopted the new constitution for Ethiopia. For the opposition parties, the adoption of a new constitution and the establishment of the FDRE signaled the determination of EPRDF to rule Ethiopia by any means necessary.

In May and June of 1995, the first national

parliamentary and regional legislators' elections were held (Wikipedia, 2006). With no real opposition parties in the electoral game, the EPRDF became the first "democratically" elected ruler of Ethiopia. The 2000 election also took place without the participation of any major opposition parties.

The EPRDF won the 2000 election by securing 90 percent of the electoral vote. In the 2005 election, the EPRDF and the opposition parties had agreed to make the 2005 election free and fair. Election laws were amended, lifting some of the legal barriers that prevented the opposition parties from full participation in the previous two elections. In one example of a change in election laws, the five-year residency requirement, which the Ethiopian government imposed on political candidates, was reduced to only six months, thus permitting exiled political leaders to return home in time for the May 2005 election. The government also agreed to provide access to government-owned television and radio stations, so that the opposition parties could introduce their political programs to the public. For the EPRDF's leadership, this was a fatal error because the opposition parties used their access to government-owned media to encourage people to talk to each other about the many problems affecting their country.

> One participant stated:
> When we saw the oppositions publicly
> criticizing EPRDF officials during the
> debate, we began to speak of politics

openly.

THE MAIN OPPOSITION PARTIES

The Coalition for Unity and Democracy (CUD)

The Coalition for Unity and Democracy (CUD) was formed in October 2004 by four political parties—All Ethiopian Unity Party (AEUP), United Ethiopian Democratic Party-Medhin (UEDP-Medhin), Ethiopian Democratic League (EDL) and Rainbow Ethiopia: Movement for Democracy and Social Justice (Kestedamena). The CUD formed in order to forge a common electoral front for the May 15, 2005 national election in Ethiopia (Wubneh, 2006). The CUD was led by Ato Hailu Shawel, and prides itself as an advocate for Ethiopian unity and for the formation of a true democratic republic in Ethiopia.

As the name of its member parties indicates, "All Ethiopian, United Ethiopian, Ethiopian, Rainbow Ethiopia" the CUD was a party that strives for unification. CUD claims to represent all Ethiopians, which is different from other parties that represent particular ethnic groups. The participants in this study agreed with CUD's claims. The participants cited Ethiopian unity as one of the most important issues that determined their party preferences. About 7 in 10 participants strongly agreed that CUD would protect the interests of all Ethiopians. About 8 in 10 study participants also strongly agreed that CUD believes in Ethiopian unity.

One participant said:

They (CUD) believe in the unity of
Ethiopia. There is only one Ethiopia,
nothing else.

The United Ethiopian Democratic Forces (UEDF)

Formed in 2003, the United Ethiopian
Democratic Forces (UEDF) was a "transitional
alliance" of 15 ethnic-based and non-ethnic-
based political parties. Dr. Merara Gudina
(chairman) and Dr. Beyene Petros (vice
chairman) led UEDF until their expulsion on
October 24, 2005.   These two leaders were
expelled by the UEDF's Central Committee
(CC) after they joined an "illegal EPRDF-
controlled Ethiopian Parliament" (UEDF press
release 2005); and they were soon replaced by
Fasika Belete, Chairman and Ayalsew Dessa,
Vice Chairman.

In post-election day Ethiopia, the transition
alliances, which the 15 political parties created
in 2003, failed to hold the parties together. In
the aftermath of the May 2005 election, the
UEDF was divided into two groups after its
central committee disagreed with a decision
made by its former party chairman and vice
chairman, Beyene Petros and Merara Gudina.
Consequently, after October 2005, two United
Ethiopian Democratic Forces exited
simultaneously: one based in Ethiopia, which is
led by the two expelled leaders and the other
one that operates outside the country, mainly

in the United States and Europe.

POST-ELECTION CRISIS AND RESPONSE

In almost any political crisis, how political leaders handle a given political impasse either relieves or aggravates the situation. Political leaders are not the only factors influencing political crises. However, political leaders do play significant roles in times of political crisis in affecting the outcome of a situation. Political crises are real testing grounds on which leaders can demonstrate their leadership abilities. The post-election-day political crisis in Ethiopia provided the ruling EPRDF and the opposition party leaders many opportunities to demonstrate their leadership skills and to overcome the political impasse.

The EPRDF Government

Since the EPRDF came to power in 1990s, the Ethiopian government attitude towards dissent has been generally undemocratic, alienating, and brutal. The government response to the post-election political crisis was no different from its response to political grievances in the past: they moved to suppress the rights of the entities that opposed them. The only time the government demonstrated some forms of tolerance was during the televised debate leading up to the May 15, 2005 national election. No top opposition party members were arrested, tortured, or killed for speaking against the government during this period.

The EPRDF had previously perceived dissent as a threat to its one-party rule, and the party had responded to such perceived dangers by mobilizing all of the legal and military forces at its disposal to suppress it. These actions have been documented by local and international human rights groups and by various news agencies.

<u>Table 1. Selected Actions taken by The Ethiopian People's Revolutionary Democratic Front (EPRDF) in Response to Political Dissent from 1991-2005</u>

Year	What Happened	Place	Parties involved	Summary of the incidents as reported	Reported By
1991	A protester killed	Addis Ababa, Ethiopia	Protesters vs. EPRDF Security Forces	"Ethiopia must stay united," the agitated demonstrators had cried. I was standing with Tigrean soldiers, who were still dressed in their ragtag rebel clothes, when they singled out one demonstrator and cornered him in front of the exterior brick wall of a church. He was a middle-aged man with a paunch and I watched him raise his hands in a gesture of submission before the soldiers shot him at close range -- once, twice, until he collapsed"	Rabbi Micha Odenheimer, an Israeli Journalist and activist was in Addis Ababa in 1991 when the EPRDF Took control of the City. He was back in Ethiopia to report on the 2005 National Election.
1994	Gonder Massacre	City of Gonder, Ethiopia	Church goers vs. EPRDF forces	Security forces who were trying to arrest Abba Amiha Eyesus, a hermit, opened fire on the crowd and 18 people were killed and 17 wounded	The Ethiopian Human Rights Council (EHRCO) January 4, 1994
1997	Attack on Labor organizatic	Addis Aba Ethiopia	Ethiopian's Teachers' Association and Confederation of Trade Unions (CETU) vs. EPRDF	EPRDF activists targeted the Ethiopian's Teachers' Association (ETA) and the Confederation of Ethiopian Trade Unions (CETU) for control while the president of ETA, Dr. Taye Wolde Semayat, started his second year in prison in May 1997. And on May 8, 1997, the	Human Rights Watch, December 9, 1997

				police shot and killed Ato Assefa Maru, his successor at the head office of ETA.	

2001	Government attacks on Universities, Civil Society	Addis Ababa	EPRDF Security forces vs. Students and Civil Society organizations	Attacks by security forces on Addis Ababa University, in Ethiopia's capital, have led to forty-one deaths, hundreds of injuries, and the detention of over two thousand students and scores of government critics since April 17.	Human Rights Watch May 10 2001
2002	Five students were killed and many arrested	Oromia state	High School Students vs. EPRDF forces	In March, high school students in several Oromiya towns staged protest marches against the regional government's educational and land policies. The state authorities declared the protests to be illegal. In the town of Shambu, the police opened fire using live ammunition when students failed to disperse and five students were killed and many arrested.	Human Rights Watch May 22, 2002
2002	The Awassa Massacre	City of Awassa, the Capita of Sidama	Farmers vs. EPRDF forces	Security agents used machine guns mounted on armored vehicles to fire into the group o unarmed farmers, killing twenty-five and injuring twenty-six. Among the dead twelve of them were children. The farmers were protesting against government decision to move regional government office to Aleta-Wondo town.	EHRCO Specia Report No. 51 June 4, 2002
2003	Abduction and Disappearance	Ethiopia	Families of the Disappeared and EPRDF Security Forces	Thirty-seven individuals have been abducted by the EPRDF security forces and their whereabouts is unknown	EHRCO Specia Report No. 61 March 21, 200:
2003	The Gambella Massacre	Gambella town, SW. Ethiopia	The Anuak ethnic community vs. EPRDF soldiers and Militias	On Dec 12 & 13, in retaliation for the killing of five Satcon construction company employees by unidentified group, the EPRDF soldiers and highlanders entered Gambella	Genocide Watch and Survivors' Rights International, Feb 25, 2004.

Year	Event	Location	Parties	Description	Source
				town and brutally raped, tortured and killed 424 Anuaks. Most of the victim were students and educated Anuaks.	EHRCO Special Report No. 72, Jan. 5, 2004
2004	Harassing the Press	Ethiopia	Ministry of Justice vs. Ethiopian Free Journalists Association (EFJA)	The Ethiopian Ministry of Justice canceled EFJA's registration as a private voluntary organization on charges that group had failed to file financial reports. This cancellation of registration prohibited the association from continuing to operate. A few weeks before the cancellation, Minister of Information Bereket Simeon accused the EFJA of undermining "responsible journalism" by opposing a government bill to regulate news reporting.	Human Rights Watch, Feb 13, 2004
2005	Massacre in Addis Ababa	Addis Ababa	Addis Ababa University Students and Addis Residents vs. EPRDF Security forces	In June 8 EPRDF security forces killed at least 36 students who came together at their campus to express their opinion about allegation of election irregularity. In November another 41 people were killed by security forces and thousands of suspected opposition parties supporters and the entire CUD leaders, journalists, human rights defenders were detained.	Amnesty International Report 2006 BBC

Table 1 shows that the EPRDF has committed kidnappings, torture, and extrajudicial killings.

Table 1 shows that the EPRDF has committed kidnappings, torture, and extrajudicial killings. Many students were expelled from universities because of their political views. Even Ethiopian political refugees in Kenya were not spared from EPRDF's security networks.

> One participant told this story:
> I was in Eastlegh (a slum in Nairobi, Kenya) when I was attacked by EPRDF selay (spy). They tried to force me into a car but I fought back and was able to escape. They stabbed me on my back. I was under UN protection and lived in a UN safe house.

More shocking, however, was the June and November 2005 killing of 193 poll protesters by EPRDF's security forces, which reflected a pattern of behavior that the EPRDF has demonstrated since 1991.

> One participant said:
> I saw a 15 years old kid get killed after the election.

> Another one claimed:
> A few distances from my house, a 9th grade student wearing his school uniform was gun down by EPRDF security forces.

> Another one reported:
> Fortunately, it was not me, but my friends. They were imprisoned in the different military camps (Awash Arba, Dedesa, Hurso and Addis Ababa). Some of

them are still imprisoned, most died during the harsh penalties and bad atmosphere of the areas and some were detained for 2 to 8 weeks.

According to an independent inquiry commission established by the Ethiopian parliament to investigate post election violence, in June and November 2005 alone about 199 Ethiopians were killed and 834 were injured. Among the civilians killed during post election violence, 19 of them were under the age of 18. Most of the killed were shot in the head or chest, which indicates the shooter may have been a member of specially trained units of the security forces (Report by the Independent Inquiry Commission, 2006).

In Ethiopia, multiparty democracy has existed in name only. No political parties other than the EPRDF were allowed to introduce legislation in the previous two parliaments. For the last 15 years, the Ethiopian parliament was used to giving the one-party state political legitimacy and a rubber stamp to its rule. However, in 2005, the opposition parties increased their seats in the Ethiopian parliament from 12 to 172, and the EPRDF response was to change the parliamentary rule in order to make it difficult for the opposition parties to participate in the policy making process (See Table 2).

Table 2. Official Results of the 2005 Ethiopia's National Election

Ethiopian People Revolutionary Democratic Front (EPRDF)	327	Coalition of Unity and Democracy (CUD)	109	Gambella People's Democratic Movement (GPDM)	3
Somali People's Democratic Party (SPDP)	24	United Ethiopian Democratic Forces (UDEF)	52	Harari National League	1
Afar National Democratic Party (ANDP)	8	Oromo Federalist Democratic Movement (OFDM)	11	Argoba Nationality Democratic Organization (ANDO)	1
Benishangul-Gumuz People's Democratic Unity Front	8			Sheko and Mezenger People's Democratic Unity Organization (SMPDUO)	1
				Independent	1
Total Seats	367	Total Seats	172	Total	7

Source: The National election Board of Ethiopia. The opposition parties have rejected the

above election results.

Following the 2005 national election, the outgoing parliament unilaterally changed the rules of the game and made a 51 percent majority necessary in order to place legislative items on the agenda. This action essentially prevented any opposition parties from introducing legislation. When the new parliament convened on October 11, 2005, most opposition leaders, particularly members of the CUD, refused to take their seats in parliament. Soon after, the government stripped parliamentary immunity from those who refused to take their seats, which then made it possible for the government to arrest elected opposition leaders during the first week of November 2005.

Thus, the EPRDF has continued to hang on to its power since 1991 by taking advantage of the courts, the parliament, and the police and military forces.

As Table 1 illustrated, an uninterrupted pattern of human rights violations have been committed by the ruling EPRDF against citizens in order to limit or exclude their participation in democratic processes. As Table 1 illustrated, the mechanism by which the EPRDF has chosen to use to limit citizens' political participation appears to be antidemocratic.

The continuing application of force by the state security agencies against unarmed civilians and political opponents seems to confirm the ruling party's desire to cling to power. On the other hand, about 8 in 10 study participants strongly agreed that CUD would do better in promoting human rights, justice and, democracy in Ethiopia than would the EPRDF.

The majority of study participants also believed that the EPRDF would not relinquish power to anyone. Of the 31 individuals who participated in this study, none of them were convinced that the EPRDF would relinquish power without violent confrontation. One participant told me: Weyane will never transfer power to anyone unless it is forced to do so. The only way to remove Weyane from power is through an armed struggle.

> Another interviewee concurred:
> As we have seen it in the 2005 election, voting alone would not remove Weyane from power. To resolve the current political crisis, Weyane must be removed by force.

> Another participant said:
> In my opinion, from the beginning, Weyane was created to destroy Ethiopia.

> Another participant said:
> What do you expect? They fought the Derg for 17 years. They sacrificed so many lives to get where they are today. Do you think they would transfer power to Kinijit i.e. CUD because they held an election? No, that will never happen. I think Kinijit leaders made a mistake. They should have

joined parliament if they want peace.

The peoples' history of Ethiopia has been and remains to be a history of resistance to oppression. The people's resistance against the rule of Colonel Mengistu Hailemariam brought down the dictator and led to the EPRDF's rise to power. As Table 2 illustrated, neither massacre nor mass detention of political opponents have ever achieved their intended goal: to silence political dissenters. Ethiopians have continued to resist the one-party rule of the EPRDF government as they did in the past.

> One participant said:
> The struggle will continue. The people are organizing themselves. We are also organizing ourselves. Within a short period of time change will come to Ethiopia.

OPPOSITIONS

Although 35 political parties were registered to seek public office in the 2005 Ethiopian national election, the "real" competition for parliamentary seats was between the ruling EPRDF and the two main opposition parties: the Coalition for Unity and Democracy (CUD) and the United Ethiopian Democratic Forces (UEDF). Between the two opposition parties, the CUD was the most favored political party by far, and its leaders were the most respected and admired for their commitment to establishing a democratic and human rights based regime in Ethiopia. For the CUD, the establishment of a united and truly democratic republic of Ethiopia remains the party's primary goal.

Throughout its election campaign, the CUD had clearly communicated its political platform to the public by focusing on essential issues such as national unity, economic development, education, human rights, corruption, land ownership rights, and the rule of law and democracy. According to one participant:
I voted for CUD and for bright future to our country according to their manifesto.

Another one declared:

I voted for CUD (Kinijit). I do have many reasons for this. One is the boring, bureaucratic and ethnic based government. The other reason is most of the political leaders in CUD are professionals unlike that of dormant EPRDF's. I know surprisingly with shame, many posted individuals with no qualifications and only because they support the ruling class and/or came from region 1(Tigray). Moreover, the academic and economic policy of CUD is nice for me. In all directions, the two parties are incompatible.

One of the most important issues cited by study participants was economic development in Ethiopia. About nine in 10 participants strongly agreed that CUD would do better in promoting equitable economic development in Ethiopia than the EPRDF.

One participant reported:

The people in the party are educated and would organize themselves for the growth of Ethiopia. Most of them are rich. They don't need the poor Ethiopians money. They will work for the improvement of the life of those poor people. It is not bad to try being lead by the party I chose, but that didn't work out.

By concentrating on issues of both local and national significance, the CUD was able to reach out and mobilize diverse groups of Ethiopians across the country. The party messages of peace, unity, and respect for human rights and human dignity had captured the attention and support of urban as well as rural Ethiopians across the country.

One participant stated:
In my opinion, Kinijit means love. It is a sign of love. The reason I love Kinijit is that its weapon is Kelem (literary means ink; Amharic expression for erudite). They only have eskirebto en woreket (pens and papers). They believe in equality. I also like professor Mesfin speech. Weyane means, a name for division and dismemberment.

Unsurprisingly, many study participants cautiously welcomed CUD's call for a nonviolent political struggle against the TPLF/EPRDF's one-party rule. Others viewed CUD's call for a nonviolent struggle against the

TPLF/EPRDF as a cover up for ethnic
cleansing.

One participant told me:
The opposition parties did incite violence.
They told the public that the Tigray people
are exploiting this country. They also told
the public that, the Tigray people are both
the government and the businessmen.
And such statements are tantamount to
attempted genocide.

Another one stated:
Kinijit tried to start ethnic conflict in
Ethiopia. My father lives in Addis Ababa.
After the election his house was targeted
by Kinijit supporter youth because he was
perceived as EPRDF supporter. They tried
to get to his house but the house has high
wall, which prevented them to jump over.

Another participant reported:
In Addis Ababa, people were talking about
sending Tigrean to Mekele (the capital of
Tigray). Set wede kebele, Tigre wede
Mekela tebelo yewera neber (literally
means: women to Kebele, Tigre to Mekele.
(Kebele is the smallest administrative
unit)

In the aftermath of the May 2005 election, the
CUD has called for nonviolent civil
disobedience. On October 10, the CUD
boycotted the Third Ethiopian Parliament after
the EPRDF refused to accept the "8-point
precondition" submitted to the prime minister

by the CUD Council (See appendix # III). On November 1, 2005, after the ruling party refused to resolve the post election political crisis through dialogue, the CUD announced a plan for a general strike. The general strike was planned to take place on November 4, 2005.

On November 2, 2005, the government began arresting CUD's leaders, members, and supporters. The rounding up of the CUD leaders by the government sparked public outrage and demonstrations, which resulted in violent confrontation between stone throwing youths and the Ethiopian military. One respondent who participated in the November protest described his involvement as follows:

> I, and those like me, do not have weapons or any defending mechanism (even no embassy was reacting [to] the government), and because of that, our last option was smooth civil disobedience/demonstration.

The government saw the November civil disobedience in Addis Ababa as a domestic insurrection, and the government flooded the city with security forces. In Addis Ababa alone, some 133 protesters and six members of the EPRDF security personnel were killed. Some 763 civilians and 71 security personnel sustained light as well as serious injuries, and 30,000 people were detained (Report by The Independent Inquiry Commission, 2006). Study participants from Addis Ababa described their reaction to the November massacre and mass arrest as follows:

"I was shocked;" "I was very upset;" "I was very angry;" "I was very sad because unexpected things happened."

> One participant stated:
> Right now, everything is not clear and many are in trouble. The situation is getting worse. So, I guess many bad things may happen here like strike or worst.

> Another participant concurred:
> At this time particularly after the CUD leaders are put in prison, the government civil cadres have been dispatched in all directions around the country. As a result, people are afraid to talk and have stopped talking politics. In addition, because of the government crackdown on the independent press, we are unable to get information other than from the government-controlled media. We listen to VOA and German Radio, but people are not discussing issues as they used to before the election. Therefore, if things continue this way, I do not see the situation improving.

Most participants also agreed that that ruling EPRDF will continue to rule Ethiopia, and the country would continue to be unstable. Some participants hope that the opposition parties take control of power by force:

> I hope the ruling class takes position by

force in the coming five years. Because almost all the top political leaders of CUD are still in prison and some of these leaders are ill and may die in prison.

Some participants also stated that ethnic division would be a serious problem for the country. One participant predicted:
There will be very serious division along ethnic lines.

Another one concurred:
It is difficult for me to guess, but people are divided along ethnic lines. They do not trust each other. Our unity is in danger unless the EPRDF is removed from power.

It was obvious that having no organized army, the police, the intelligence or the court on their sides, the options left for the opposition parties were either to stage a protest or to find a peaceful end to the crisis. To that end, the CUD and UEDF wrote to the late prime minister requesting that they wanted to resolve the crisis peacefully (Petros and Nega, letter 2005).

With the help of the Ambassadors' Donors Group several attempts were made to resolve the conflict peacefully, but none has produced positive results. Even the June 10, 2005 joint declaration did not prevent the November massacre of unarmed civilians by government forces and the crack down on the opposition leaders. The declaration was signed by the CUD, UEDF, and the EPRDF to "re-affirm" the parties' commitment to the "successful and peaceful conclusion of the electoral process (Joint Declaration June 10, 2005)."

In addition, the refusal of CUD leaders to take their seats in parliament made the opposition parties more vulnerable to government harassment. In the end, CUD's political activities in Ethiopia have been effectively eliminated after the government accused the party of domestic insurrection and arrested its entire leadership. Consequently, the leaders of a once promising national political party were sent to prison or are in exile.

But why did the CUD leaders decided not to join parliament? According to one participant, the party actually wanted to join parliament as long as the government was willing to accept the 8-point precondition.

We could have entered parliament if the government has accepted the 8-point precondition. The letter was sent to the Prime Minister but immediately after that, the government began taking measure against the oppositions.

Some study participants however believe that CUD was under pressure from the Ethiopian expatriate community to reject the election outcome; and other participants stated that CUD leaders were misinform by the European Union Observation Mission about election results. One participant stated:

Those who contributed greatly to the post

election crisis are the EU, the Ethiopians who live abroad, and the political parties. I believe that the Ethiopians who live in the United States put pressure on the opposition parties to reject the election results and also not to work along with the EPRDF.

> Another participant concurred:

> In my opinion, the number one source of our post election problem was the European Union (EU) Observation Mission. EU leaked information to the opposition parties. They told the opposition parties, you have won the election.

It has been a tradition for democratic regimes to resolve internal political conflict nonviolently. Elections are part of settling political conflict by peaceful means by allowing the voters to judge. When the election became a source of violent confrontation, the question became, what do the political players and their supporters have to say about it?

I asked my participants what factors they thought contributed to Ethiopia's post election political crisis. From the responses I gathered, I learned that the majority of the people I talked to believe that for the most part "Weyane," i.e. the TPLF/EPRDF, was responsible for the 2005 post election political crisis because they stole the election from CUD. They are also convinced that the EPRDF would not peacefully transfer power to any other political party.

Interestingly, when I asked participants to talk about their wish and what they want to see happen in Ethiopia, they expressed their wishes in positive terms:

> I want to see political change and a free country.

> Another participant stated:
> I want to see a democratic government set up in Ethiopia.

> Another one stated:
> I wish to see people to be free and to be part of a political movement and also live peacefully.

The majority of study participants also wished to see a *Fitehawi Mengist* (i.e. a just government). One participant said:
I want to see an all-inclusive and *fitehawi Mengist* in Ethiopia.

> Another one concurred:
> I wish to see a government that administers justice and provides development to its citizens.

> Another one stated:
> I want a government that maintains our unity and leads us. I want a government, which does not believe in ethnicity; and a government that views all citizens as one and equal.

Furthermore, I learned that the issues of peace, unity, equality, economic development, education and ethnicity were very important subjects to the study participants. One study participant told me how he dreams about:

> ...living in a peaceful country where ethnicity would no longer be part of the national political discourse.

> Another participant stated:
> I want a democratic government. I want discrimination to stop. I want especially ethnocentrism to disappear from our country.

Concerning equality, I heard from the participants, who talked about how they have been treated as second-class citizens in their own countries because of their ethnicities. One participant told me that:

> What I want is, I want to live in a country where people believe in equality, live together and also a country that is not depending on agriculture. I want democracy and development.

In addition, many participants were concerned about EPRDF's education policy, which cuts high school education short at tenth grade as counterproductive to youth development. About 6 in 10 participants strongly agreed that CUD would do better in providing better education for all Ethiopians than the EPRDF.

One participant said:

> They (CUD) will correct the education and other policies that are not suited for the growth of the country.

Participants were asked to identify and rank the top five important issues in determining their party preferences. The participants cited economic development as their number one issue followed by Ethiopian unity/human rights/democracy (equal numbers of votes), protecting the interest of all Ethiopians (as opposed to particular ethnic groups), education, and change in leadership.

Based on data collected from study participants, the following points can be made:

- ✓ Promoting economic development in Ethiopia was a very important issue to participants and they viewed CUD as a well-qualified party that would accelerate the economic development of their country.
- ✓ Maintaining the unity of Ethiopia was equally important as promoting democracy and protecting human rights.
- ✓ The Ethiopian people still view the EPRDF as TPLF. The public doesn't see EPRDF as a coalition of four political parties. Instead, they see EPRDF and TPLF as the same political party: Weyane.
- ✓ The public still does not believe that the EPRDF is a government that represents

and stands for all Ethiopians. They still
see the government as almost as an
occupying power that is there to protect
the interest of the ethnic Tigre.
- ✓ The public remains doubtful about
  whether democratic transitions would
  ever take place in Ethiopia as long as the
  EPRDF is in power.
- ✓ Almost everyone I spoke to, with an
  exception of a few, hoped to see a
  peaceful settlement to the post election
  political crisis.

ETHIOPIAN DIASPORA AND DONORS

Similar to the June and November
spontaneous protests in Ethiopia, the
Ethiopian communities abroad also
spontaneously reacted to the post election
political killing by organizing a huge "peace
rally" in major North American, European,
Australian, and South African cities. The
protesters condemned the killing of unarmed
civilians by the EPRDF security forces. They
demanded that western countries withdraw
support of the Ethiopian government.

I attended some of these rallies in Washington,
D.C. I saw people carrying the Ethiopian flag
along with the U.S. flag, along with blown up
pictures of those who were victims of the June
and November massacres. The protesters
demanded the Bush administration to speak
out against the massacre in Ethiopia. They also
demanded democracy for Ethiopia.

In front of the White House the protesters
shouted:

> President Bush: Democracy for Ukraine,
> democracy for Georgia, democracy for
> Ethiopia too. President Bush, stop the
> massacre in Ethiopia. President Bush,
> Meles is a terrorist. He is terrorizing the
> Ethiopian people. Our mothers, our
> fathers, our brothers, and our sisters are
> dying in Ethiopia. President Bush, where
> is your compassion?

Beside public demonstrations, Ethiopian-
Americans have also advocated on behalf of
Ethiopians at home in the U.S. Congress. As a
result, on June 27, 2006, the U.S. House
International Relations Committee approved a
comprehensive bill authored by Representative
Chris Smith of New Jersey. The bill—the
Ethiopia Freedom, Democracy and Human
Rights Advancement Act of 2006 (HR 5680)—
includes provisions that call for the release of
all political prisoners. The bill also provides
support for the advancement of human rights,
democracy, and judicial independence,
freedom of the press, peacekeeping, capacity
building, and economic development in
Ethiopia. HR 5680 also denies visas to "any
official of the government of Ethiopia who has
been involved in giving orders to use lethal
force against peaceful demonstrators in
Ethiopia. (H.R. 5680).

In Europe, Australia, Canada, and South

Africa, Ethiopians have also put enormous pressure on officials of these countries to use their influence against the Ethiopian government. For example, former Prime Minister Tony Blair of United Kingdom was pressured by the Ethiopian community in Europe to suspend a Ł50 million direct budgetary support his government provides to the Ethiopian government. The World Bank also cut its direct budgetary aid to Ethiopia for one year.

The spontaneous and global mobilization of the Ethiopian expatriate communities in post election period has been unprecedented. Modern communication technologies such as the cell phone and the Internet played a very prominent role in connecting the Ethiopian exile communities to events that were taking place in Ethiopia. During the post-election crisis, many Ethiopians got first hand accounts of the crisis from their family and friends through cell phones and email. Getting firsthand information through email and phone calls made the political conflict back home even closer and more significant to the Ethiopian exile communities. It was the availability and access to these technologies, as well as the instant flow of information between the old and new homes of the expatriate communities, which made it possible for them to play a significant role in post election Ethiopia from abroad.

CONCLUSIONS

The post election political crisis in Ethiopia was a result of the ruling party's sturdy assertion of electoral victory ahead of the NEBE, an agency that was solely responsible for officially announcing the election results, along with the government decision to ban public protests. The EPRDF executive committee's decision to declare victory just a day after election day unnerved the opposition parties and their supporters and ultimately sparked a post election political crisis. In the end, the conflict brought immense suffering to thousands of Ethiopians.

As this study illustrated, the repressive actions taken by the EPRDF against protesters in June and November of 2005 as well as its prior despotic measures applied against political dissidents seems to suggest that the ruling party is neither ready nor willing to share power with opposition political parties. Thus, creating a democratic and human rights regime in Ethiopia appears not to be a priority for the ruling party.

On the other hand, the roles the opposition parties played during the crisis were minimal. Aside from threatening to take it to the street, no opposition political parties called for public demonstrations or the use of force to overthrow the government. Instead, the opposition parties tried to resolve the crisis peacefully through negotiation. They expressed their willingness to join parliament as long as the government met certain conditions. These conditions were:

> ➤ The legal system must be able to operate independently without any coercion from the ruling party.
> ➤ All forms of media must be free and available to all political parties.
> ➤ Opposition party offices that had been closed [by the government] should be opened.

In my judgment, the government could have met these conditions if the ruling party was interested in resolving the political crisis peacefully. Sadly, the government chose to use coercive power instead.

The CUD's reliance on public participation in the political decision making process may have also contributed to its own demise. The refusal of the CUD's leadership to join parliament may have escalated the conflict. It may also have provided a pretext for the government to destroy the party. Moreover, by taking unrealistic approaches and steps in dealing with a political party known for its history of deceit and manipulation, the CUD leaders may have missed a historic opportunity to take the Ethiopian people one-step forward toward freedom and democracy.

RECOMMENDATIONS

It is in the interest of both the EPRDF and the opposition parties to find workable and realistic political solutions for the political crisis in Ethiopia. The time to look for a common ground is now and a common ground can only be found through dialogue. There cannot be a legal or military solution for Ethiopia's political problems. The only way Ethiopia can be politically stable is if the leaderships of both the EPRDF and the opposition parties open their hearts and ears to listen to one another as friends and colleagues, instead of viewing each other as enemies.

The past is the past, and focusing on the future is of paramount importance for the betterment of all Ethiopians. In dialogue, it is imperative to focus on the future as opposed to the past because the past can be divisive and an impediment to progress. Thus, the following should be done as quickly as possible in order to overcome the ongoing political crisis:

> - The Prime Minister should immediately ask the Ethiopian parliament for a legislation that would allow him to put together a team of Ethiopian elders and experts who do not have any political affiliation with either EPRDF or the opposition parties and to serve as a third party mediator.
> - The Parliament should hold both closed and open hearings to approve or reject the prime minister appointees. The team should consist of native Ethiopians. The legislatures also should provide legal as well as financial backing of the teams in order to accomplish its task, which would be to serve as third-party mediators between the EPRDF and the

opposition parties.

- ➢ Strengthening democratic institutions in Ethiopia is of paramount importance if democracy is to succeed in Ethiopia. The older democracies such as those of the United States and the European Union can do a lot to help Ethiopia build democratic institutions. Technical assistance from the United States and Europe, along with political pressure on the ruling party could make a huge difference in strengthening democratic institutions in Ethiopia. It may also politically stabilize the country and avert possible civil war.

APPLICATIONS OF THE RESEARCH

This study connected the dots and identified patterns by looking closely at the actions taken by political actors for the purpose of making sense of Ethiopia's post election political crisis. It also went further to describe and analyze some of the actions taken by the ruling party against political dissenters since 1991. The study also illustrated how Ethiopia's democratic institutions still exhibit a lack of institutional maturity and remained to be incapable of operating independent of the executive branch of the government and the party, which controls it. More importantly, the study attempted to capture the thoughts and feelings of Ethiopians both at home abroad and provided them with opportunities to tell their stories.

Lesson learned from this study is that promoting election-centered democracy without the establishment of independent democratic institutions such as an independent legal system has threatened the stability of Ethiopia's emerging democracy. For those governmental and non-governmental organizations that have been working in Ethiopia to promote democracy and the rule of law for over a decade may need to reevaluate their strategies. They also need to recognize that a free election is not effective in and of itself.

As the government's response to post election crisis indicated, there appeared to be no distinction between the state institutions and the ruling party. No branches of Ethiopian government seemed to function independently of the ruling party. The executive, legislative, and judicial branches of the government have repeatedly violated or ignored Ethiopia's1994 constitution, which happened to be written by the same political party that has been in power since the birth of democracy in Ethiopia. The rule of law has been seriously undermined by the very institutions, which supposed to uphold and enforce the law. For a democratic system to take root in Ethiopia, the establishment of independent democratic institutions may be as important as regular elections.

Finally I hope this study has provided some insight as to why the EPRDF failed to conduct clean, transparent, free and fair elections since they came to power in 1991. I also hope the study would encourages dialogue among the many stakeholders and also mobilize resources and technical expertise to strengthen Ethiopia's fragile democratic institutions and avert the country's possible return to the familiar terrain of "dominant power politics" of the Cold War era and one-party rule.

SUGGESTIONS FOR FUTURE RESEARCH

The political history of Ethiopia has been a history of regional rivalry for domination. Since 1991, a new and intensely upgraded dimension of rivalry was added to the old regional conflict: an ethnic dimension. Prior to the accession of EPRDF to power, there were 14 provinces in Ethiopia. Today there are only nine linguistically defined, ethnic-based federal states. Out of the newly created states, only the state of Tigray retained its original shape, and the rest were patched together to form the remaining eight federal states: the states of Afar, Amhara, Benishangul-Gumuz, Gambella, Harrari, Oromia, Somalia, and Southern Nations. As this study illustrated, under EPRDF rule, the intensity and magnitude of interethnic political conflict in Ethiopia has been overwhelming. I believe further research in the following areas may shade light on the impacts of inventing and imposing individual identity and creating ethnic homeland based solely on language in a multi-ethnic and multilingual Ethiopia.

Interethnic relations and minority rights since the 1990s:
To what extent does the creation of linguistically defined ethnic homelands in a multiethnic society like Ethiopia affect interethnic relations?
On shimagela (Elders):
To what extent does the traditional ways of resolving political conflict in Ethiopia applicable today?
Foreign Aid and Democratization in Ethiopia:
 To what extent does foreign aid promote or hinder democratization process in Ethiopia?
On Ethiopian expatriate communities:
What influences do exile and home-based political parties have on Ethiopians at home and abroad?

LIST OF ABBREVIATIONS

AEUP	All Ethiopian Unity Party
ANDM	Amhara National Democratic Movement
CUD	Coalition for Unity and Democracy
EFFORT	Endowment Fund for the Rehabilitation of Tigray
EDL	Ethiopian Democratic League
EHRCO	Ethiopian Human Rights Council
EPLF	Eritrean People's Liberation Front
EPRDF	Ethiopian People's Revolutionary Democratic Front
FDRE	Federal Democratic Republic of Ethiopia
NEBE	National Election Board of Ethiopia
ODPO	Oromo People's Democratic Organization
OLF	Oromo Liberation Front
SEPM	Southern Ethiopian People's Democratic Movement
TGE	Transitional Government of Ethiopia
TPLF	Tigray People's Liberation Front
UEDF	United Ethiopian Democratic Forces

Selected Bibliography

Abbink, J. (1997). Ethnicity and constitutionalism in
contemporary Ethiopia. Journal of African
Law, vol. 41, no. 2, pp. 159-174.

Abubakar, D. (2001). Ethnic identity, democracy,
and the Future of the African state: Lessons
from Nigeria. African Issues. vol. 29, no. 1/2
pp. 31-36.

Alelmu, T. (2005). Open letter to Professor
Christopher Clapham. Retrieved October 6,
2006
fromhttp://www.mfa.gov.et/view_commentari
es/Open%20Letter%20%to%20Christopher/%
20Clapham.htm.

Amnesty International (2006). Annual Report
Africa: Ethiopia. Retrieved October 6, 2006
from http://web.amnesty.org/report2006/eth-
Summary-eng.

Anonymous, "Crime and Nourishment in Ethiopia:
American and European Taxpayers' Money at
Work," Ethiopian Review. Available URL:
http://ethiopianreview.homestead.com/Crime
_Nourishment01012006.pdf.

Atsbeha, T. and Kahsay, B. (2002). Two groups of
the TPLF and two issues of Ethiopia. Retrieved
October 6, 2006 from
http://www.ethiomedia.com/what_is_tpfl.htm
l.

Balsvik, R. (1985). Haile Sellassie's students: The

intellectual and social background to revolution, 1952-1977. Ed. Harold G. Marcus. East Lansing, Michigan: African Studies Center.

BBC (June 6, 2005). Arrests for Ethiopia poll protest. Retrieved October 6, 2006 from: http://news.bbc.co.uk/1/hi/world/africa/4613741.stm.

Belai, A. Tigrai vs. Kinijit: A dialogue with Prof. Donald Levine. Retrieved October 6, 2006 from http://www.addisvoice.com/Resources/abrahab.pdf.

Berhe, K. The tyrant defying the will of the people. Retrieved October 6, 2006 from http://www.ethiomedia.com/arepress/tyrannical_defiance_four.html.

__________. (2005). Ethiopia: Democratization and Unity. Muenster: Verlaghaus Monsenstein & Vannerdat.

Blustein, P. (May 26, 2006). World Bank resumes Ethiopian assistance. The Washington Post, p. D05.

Bratton, M. and Posner, N.D. (1999). A first look at second elections in Africa, with illustrations from Zambia." In Joseph, Richard, ed. State, Conflict, and Democracy in Africa. Boulder, CO and London, UK: Lynne Reinner Publishers. pp 377-407.

Cardoso, F. H. (2005). Scholarship and diplomacy. Journal of Democracy. vol. 16, no. 2. pp.5-12.

Carothers, Thomas. "The End of the Transition Paradigm." Journal of Democracy, Volume 13, Number 1: 2002

Carter Center (September 15, 2005). Final statement on the Carter Center observation of the Ethiopia 2005 national elections. Retrieved October 6, 2006 from http://www.cartercenter.org/documents/2199.pdf

Clapham, C. (November 7, 2005). Comments on the Ethiopian crisis. Retrieved October 6, 2006 from http://www.mediaethiopia.com/Election2005/ChristopherClapham_CommentsonEthiopiaCrisis.htm.

Coalition for Unity and Democracy (May 20, 2005). CUD North American office. Retrieved October 6, 2006 from http://www.kestedemena.org/documents.cudpressrelease/052005.pdf

Constitution of the Federal Democratic Republic of Ethiopia (1994). Retrieved October 6, 2006 from http://www.ethiopar.net/english/cnstiotn/consttn.htm

Crisis Group (July 11, 2005). Counter-terrorism in Somalia: Losing hearts and minds. Africa

Report No. 11. Retrieved October 6, 2006 from
http://www.crisisgroup.org/liberary/documen
ts/africa/horn-of-africa/095-counter-
terrorism-in-somalia.pdf

Dahl, Robert A. (1971). Polyarchy: Participation and
opposition. New Haven: Yale University Press.

Diamond, L. & Plattner, M.F. (1996). The global
resurgence of democracy. Second Edition.
Baltimore and London: The Johns Hopkins
University Press.

Diamond, L. (1999). Developing democracy: Toward
consolidation. Baltimore and London: The
Johns Hopkins University Press.

EHRCO (Ethiopian Human Rights Council).
(January 14, 1994). The human rights situation
in Ethiopia. Second report. Retrieved October
6, 2006 from
http://www.ethiopians.com/repo2.html

________. (June 4, 2002). Serious human rights
violations in Awassa and its environs. Special
report No. 51. Retrieved October 6, 2006 from
http://www.ehrco.org/Reroprts/Special51.pdf.

________. (March 21, 2003). For the immediate
disclosure of the whereabouts of people who
have been abducted and disappeared. Special
report no. 61. Retrieved October 6, 2006 from
http://www.ehrco.org/Reports/Special61.pdf.
________. (January 5, 2004). A ferocious attack
committed in Gambella region. Special report
No. 72. Retrieved October 6, 2006 from

http://www.ehrco.org/Reports/Special72.pdf.

________. (December 6, 2005). No human rights =
No democracy. Special report no. 90. Retrieved
October 6, 2006 from
http://www.ehrco.org/Reports/Special90.pdf.

________. (January 12, 2006). Human rights are not
respected=There is no democracy. Special
report no. 92. Retrieved October 6, 2006 from:
http://www.ehrco.org/Reports/Special892.pdf
.

________. (October 17, 2005). Human rights
violation committed against members and
supporters of the opposition parities should be
stopped. Special report no. 89. Retrieved
October 6, 2006 from
http://www.ehrco.org/Reports/Special89.pdf.

EPRDF Organs.Behagerachen Selam Ena Lemat
Mederader Ayechalem. Retrieved October 6,
2006 from
http://eprdforgans.org/ad/p_folder/PDFfiles/
Magazines/PM-Inte_sep98.pd.pdf

________________. Yeamesth Haylochen Metages
Yemanechelebet Dereja lay Tedersuwal.
Retrieved October 6, 2006 from
http://eprdforgans.org/EPRDF_doc/Articles/l
ast_fact.pdf

________________.(Meskerem 15, 1997 Ethiopian
Calander). Tekawamiwoch Yejemeruten
Yedebebekosh Chewata Manenem
Selemaytekem Wede Selam Aktach

Endemelesu Bedegami Asasebalehu. Retrieved October 6, 2006 from http://eprdforgans.org/EPRDF_doc/Articles/PDFart/PM_.pdf

__________________. Editorial. November 5, 2005. Fighting terrorism and standing guard for Ethiopia. Retrieved October 6, 2006 from http://eprdforgans.org/EPRDF_doc/Articles/gaurd_Ethiopia.htm

EPRDF Organs (October 28, 2005). The government desirous to hand over the Addis Ababa administration to the opposition. Retrieved October 6, 2006 from http://eprdforgans.org/EPRDF-doc/Articles/Gov-desirous.htm

______.October 17, 2005. Interview with Prime Minister Meles Zenawi. Retrieved October 6, 2006 from http://eprdforgans.org/EPRDF_doc/Articles/pminte_19Oct.htm.

Eshete, A. (1993). Implementing human rights and a democratic constitution in Ethiopia. Issue: A Journal of Opinion. vol. 21, No. 1/2 pp. 8-13.

(February 19, 2006). Ethiopia's CUDP MP's divided over how to deal with ruling party. Sudan Tribune. Retrieved October 6, 2006 from: http://www.sudantribune.com/article.php3?id_article=14153.

(June 2005) Ethiopia 'in danger' after deaths. BBC 9. Retrieved October 6, 2006 from

http://news.bbc.co.uk.1/hi/world/africa/4074
822.stm#.

EU EOME (European Union Election Observation
Mission Ethiopia). Ethiopia Legislative
Elections 2005 European Union Election
Observation Mission Final Report. Retrieved
October 6, 2006 from
http://www.ethioforum.org/images/FinalRepo
rt.pdf.

___________. (May 17, 2005). Preliminary
statement. Retrieved October 6, 2006 from
http://europa.eu.int/comm/external_relations
/humanrighs/eu_election_ass_observ/ethiopi
a/pre_stat_17-05-05.pdf.

___________. (August 25, 2005). Preliminary
statement on the election appeals process: The
re-run of elections and the Somali regional
elections. Retrieved October 6, 2006 from
http:www.ethiomedia.com/fastpress/eu_press
_release.pdf.

Genocide Watch and Survivors' Rights
International. (February 25, 2004). Today in
the day of killing Anuaks: Crime against
humanity, acts of genocide and ongoing
atrocities against the Anuak people of Southern
Ethiopia. Retrieved October 6, 2006 from
http://www.survirorsrightsinternational.org/p
dfs/ANUAKREP.pdf

Gills, John R. (1994). Memory and identity: The
history of a relationship. In Gill, J, (Ed.).
Commemorations: The politics of national

identity. Princeton, New Jersey: Princeton
University Press. pp. 3-24.

Glaser, B.G. and Strauss, A.L.(1967). The discovery
of grounded theory. Aldine Transaction:
Chicago.

Harbeson, J.W. (1998). A bureaucratic authoritarian
regime: Is Ethiopia democratic? Journal of
Democracy. vol. 9, no. 4. pp. 62-69.

__________________. (2005). Ethiopia's extended
transition. Journal of Democracy. vol. 16.no.
October. pp. 144-158.

Henze, P. B. (November 14, 2005). Comments on
comments. Retrieved October 6, 2006 from
http://www.aigaforum.com/commentsoncom
ments.htm.

_______________. (1998). A political success story: Is
Ethiopia democratic? Journal of Democracy.
vol. 9.no. 4. pp. 40-54.

Hoaglin, D.C., & et al. (1982). Data for Decisions.
Cambridge Massachusetts: Abt Books

HR 5680. (2006). Ethiopia freedom, democracy and
human rights advancement act of 2006.
Retrieved October 6, 2006 from
http://frwebgate.access.gpo.gov/cgi-
bin/getdoc.cgi?dbname=109-cong-
bills&docid.text.pdf.

Human Rights Watch (1997). Ethiopia: The

curtailment of rights. vol. 9.no. 8. December
Retrieved October 6, 2006 from
http://www.hrw.org/reports/1997/ethiopia/Et
hio97d.htm

______. (May 10, 2001). Ethiopia: Government
attacks universities, civil society. Retrieved
October 6, 2006 from
http://hrw.org/press/2001/10/ethiopia-1017-
ltr.htm.

______. (May 22, 2002). Ethiopia: Halt crackdown on
Oromo students. Retrieved October 6, 2006
from
http://hrw.org/english/docs/2002/05/22/ethi
opia.3993.htm.

______. (February 13, 2004). Ethiopia: Stop
harassing journalists' group. Retrieved October
6, 2006 from
http://hrw.org/english/docs/2004/02/13/ethi
opia7347.htm.

________.(June 10, 2005). Joint declaration by
UEDF, CUD, EPRDF on the NEBE complaints
review and investigation process. Retrieved
October 6, 2006 URL:
http://www.hebret.com/press-
release/JointDeclaration061005eng.pdf.

Huntington, S.P. (1996). Democracy's third wave. In
Diamond, L. and Plattner, M.F. (Eds.). The
Global Resurgence of Democracy. Baltimore
and London: Johns Hopkins University Press.
p, 3-25.

Huntington, Samuel P. (1991). The Third Wave: Democratization in the Late Twentieth Century. Norman: University of Oklahoma Press.

Joint communiqué by CUDP and UEDF. Retrieved October 6, 2006 from http://www.kestedemena.org/pressreleases/JointPressrelease092905eng.pdf.

Joireman, S. (1997). Opposition politics and ethnicity in Ethiopia: We will all go down together. The Journal of Modern African Studies. vol. 35. no. 3. pp. 387-407.

Joseph, R. (1998). Africa, 1990-1997: From Abertura to closure. Journal of Democracy. vol. 2. no. 2. pp. 3-17.

_______________. (1999). State, conflict, and democracy in Africa. In Joseph, R.(Ed.). State, conflict, and democracy in Africa. Boulder, CO and London UK: Lynne Reinner Publishers. pp. 3-14.

_______________. (1998). Oldspeak vs. newspeak. Journal of Democracy. vol. 9. no. 4. pp. 55-61.

Kant, I. (2003).To perpetual peace: A philosophical sketch. Translated by Humphrey, T. Indianapolis and Cambridge: Hackett Publishing Company.

Keller, E.J. (1995). The ethnogenesis of the Oromo nation and its implications for politics in

Ethiopia. The Journal of Modern African Studies vol. 33. no. 4. pp. 621-634.

Kinijit Manifesto. (2006). Unofficial Translation, Version 1.0

Lacey, M. (November 14, 2005). Ethiopia's capital, once promising, finds itself in crisis. The New York Times. Retrieved October 6, 2006 from http:www.nytimes.com/2005/11/14/internatio nal/Africa/14ethiopia.html?page wanted=print.

Leftwich, A. (1996). Democracy and development: Theory and practice. Cambridge: Polity Press.

Lijphart, A. (1999). Patterns of democracy: Government forms and performance in thirty-six countries. New Haven, CT and London UK: Yale University Press.

Lyons, T. (1996). Closing the transition: The May 1995 elections in Ethiopia. The Journal of Modern African Studies. vol. 34 no. 1 pp. 121-142.

__________________. (2006). Ethiopia in 2005: The beginning of a transition? Retrieved October 6, 2006 from http://www.csis.org.

Mazzetti, M. (June 7, 2006). Efforts by CIA fail in Somalia, officials charge. The New York Times.

Memorandum of understanding for freedom and democracy in Ethiopia (May 2006). Retrieved October 6, 2006 from http://www.addisvoice.com/Resources/ADF-memorandum-of-understanding.pdf

Merriam, S. B. (1988). Case study in research
    education: A qualitative approach. Jossey-Bass
    Publishers: San Francisco and London.

Miles, M.B. & Huberman, A. (1994). Qualitative
    Data Analysis. Second Edition. SAGE
    Publications: Thousand Oaks, London and New
    Delhi.

Ministry of Information (August 27, 2005). The
    factual truths of election 2005 could not have
    become concealed by hate and deceptive
    favoritism. Retrieved October 6, 2006 from
    http://www.waltainfo.com/conflict/BasicFacts
    /2005/Aug/state3.htm.

Moss, T. J. (1995). U.S. policy and democratization
    in Africa: The limits of liberal universalism.
    The Journal of Modern African Studies. vol.33.
    no. 2. pp. 189-209.

National Electoral Board of Ethiopia (NEBE).
    Retrieved October 6, 2006 from
    http://www.electionsethiopia.org.

NEBE Consolidated election law of Ethiopia
    including the 2005 amendments. (unofficial
    translation). Retrieved October 6, 2006 from:
    http://www.electionsethiopia.org/PDF/Consol
    idated%20Election%20Laws%20(1995%20and
    %202005)%20unofficial%20version.pdf.

Nega, B.(2005). Ethiopia's struggle for democracy.
    Retrieved October 6, 2006 from

http://www.nazret.com/php/uploadnews/sear
ch.php?misc=search&subaction=showfull&id.

O'Donnell, G. & Schmitter,, P.C. (1986).
Transitions from authoritarian rule: Tentative
conclusions about uncertain democracies.
Baltimore and London: The Johns Hopkins
University Press.

Odenheimer, M. (December 18, 2005). A dream
defiled: The betrayal of Ethiopia's democracy.
The Washington Post, p. B04. Retrieved
October 6, 2006 from
http://www.washingtonpost.com/wp-
dyn/content/article/2005/12/17/AR20051217
00013_2.html.

Paxton, R.O. (2005). The anatomy of fascism. New
York: Vintage Books

Petros, Beyene & Nega, Berhanu (2005, Letter). Le
Kibur Ato Meles Zenawi Ye Ethiopia
Democrasiyawi Republic Mengist Teklay
Minister. Retrieved October 6, 2006 from
http://www.aeup/new/static/meles_080505.p
df.

Rawls, J.(2001). Justice as fairness: A restatement.
Edited by Erin Kelly. Cambridge and London:
The Belknap Press of Harvard University Press.

Report of the Federal Police Commission to the
House of People Representatives. (2005).
Retrieved October 6, 2006 from
http://eprdforgans.org/EPRDF_doc/articles/f
ed_polireport.htm.

Report by The Independent Inquiry Commission to the House of Peoples' Representatives on the violence in Addis Ababa and some other parts of our country. (October 2006). Retrieved November 1, 2006 from http:www.ethiopar.net

Sartori, G. (1987). The theory of democracy revisited. Chatham, New Jersey: Chatham House Publishers.

Sharansky, N. (2004). The case for democracy: The power of freedom to overcome tyranny and terror. Public Affairs. Perseus Books Group, USA.

Sibhatu, S. (2005). The Ethiopian politics in the coming five years. Retrieved October 6, 2006 from http://www.waltainfo.com/Analysis/2005/Dec/7843.htm.

Sklar, R.L. (1997). Development and democracy. Comparative Studies in Society and History. vol. 29. no. 4 pp. 686-714.

__________________. (1983). Democracy in Africa. African Studies Review. vol. 26. no. 3/4. pp. 11-24.

Smith, L.M. (1978). An Evolving Logic of Participant Observation, Educational Ethnography and Other Case Studies. In L. Shulman (ed), Review of Research in Education. Chicago: Peacock.

Stake, R.E. (1995). The art of case study research. CA: Thousand Oaks, London: UK, New Delhi: Sage Publications.

Submission to the 38th Ordinary Session of the African Commission on Human and Peoples' Rights, Banjul, Cambia (November 2005). Available URL: www. Achpr.org/English/communiqués/communique38_en.htm.

Terfa, S. (2006). If not now, when? If not us who? Retrieved October 6, 2006 from URL:http:// www.mediaethimedia.com/Election2005/Ifnot usWho_ProfessorSolomonTerfa_Jan2006.htm .

UEDF Press Release (October 24, 2005). Retrieved October 6, 2006 from http://www.hebret.com/UEDF-pressreleaseonDrBeyene&Merera.pfd

Unitarian Universalist Association of Congregations. (2002). The power of nonviolence: Writing by advocated of peace. Boston: Beacon Press

Walta (September 2, 2006). Interview with Prime Minister Meles Zenawi. Retrieved October 6, 2006 from http://www.waltainfo.com/AmNews/1997/26S en97/Meles-Interview.pdf.

________. (Genbot 14, 1997). "Keeyeadeg Sera Asfestame Kometa Yetesete Derejetawi Meglech." Available URL: http://www.waltainfo.com/EPRDF_final.pdf

Van de Walle, N. (2001). African Economy and the Politics of Permanent Crisis, 1979-1999. Cambridge: Cambridge University Press.

Vestal, T. (May 19, 2006). Ethiopia: current situation, possible solutions. Retrieved October 6, 2006 from http://www.ethiomedia.com/carepress/theodo r_vestal_ethiopia.html

Wikipedia, the free encyclopedia. Retrieved October 6, 2006 from http://en.wikipedia.org/wiki/Rule_of_law
WoldeMariam, A. (October 4, 2005). Perspectives on the EPRDF & the May 2005 Elections. Retrieved October 6, 2006 from http://www.ethiomedia.com/fastpress/perspec tives.pdf.

Wolde-Mariam, Mesfin. (2005). "Force Never Disproves Truth." Available URL: http://www.ethiomedia.com/fastpress/mesfin _woldemariam_on_zenawi_letter.html.

Wrong, M. (July 4, 2005). A crisis of leadership. Retrieved October 6, 2006 from http://www.newstatesman.com/World/20050 7040006

Wubneh, Amoraw. (2006). The difference between Kinijit And TPLF (Tigray People's Liberation Front). Retrieved October 6, 2006 from http://www.kinijit.org/content.asp?contentid= 1529

"Ye kinijit Le andenet and Le democracy Ye mercha

Manifesto, 1997" (Ethiopian Calendar), Addis Ababa, Ethiopia. (Amharic).

Young, J. (1997). Peasant revolution in Ethiopia: The Tigray people's Liberation Front 1975-1999. London: Cambridge University Press.

Zenawi, Meles. (2005). Easy to remove the garbage that has covered lumps of truth. Retrieved October 6, 2006 from http://www. Walt info.com/conflict/BasicFacts/2005/Aug/state4 .htm.

_______________. (March 28, 2006). Report presented by Prime Minister Meles Zenawi to the House of Peoples' Representatives of the Federal Democratic Republic of Ethiopia. Retrieved October 6, 2006 from http://www.waltainfo.com/currentIssues/Mar /Report.htm.